J

D0899272

Motorcycles

Harley-Davidson

Dash!
LEVELED READERS
An Imprint of Abdo Zoom • abdopublishing.com

2

Dash!
LEVELED READERS

Level 1 – Beginning
Short and simple sentences with familiar words or patterns for children who are beginning to understand how letters and sounds go together.

Level 2 – Emerging
Longer words and sentences with more complex language patterns for readers who are practicing common words and letter sounds.

Level 3 – Transitional
More developed language and vocabulary for readers who are becoming more independent.

abdopublishing.com

Published by Abdo Zoom, a division of ABDO, PO Box 398166, Minneapolis, Minnesota 55439.
Copyright © 2019 by Abdo Consulting Group, Inc. International copyrights reserved in all countries.
No part of this book may be reproduced in any form without written permission from the publisher.
Dash!™ is a trademark and logo of Abdo Zoom.

Printed in the United States of America, North Mankato, Minnesota.
052018
092018

Photo Credits: Alamy, Getty Images, iStock, Shutterstock
Production Contributors: Kenny Abdo, Jennie Forsberg, Grace Hansen, John Hansen
Design Contributors: Dorothy Toth, Neil Klinepier

Library of Congress Control Number: 2017960622

Publisher's Cataloging in Publication Data

Names: Murray, Julie, author.
Title: Harley-Davidson / by Julie Murray.
Description: Minneapolis, Minnesota : Abdo Zoom, 2019. | Series: Motorcycles |
    Includes online resources and index.
Identifiers: ISBN 9781532123030 (lib.bdg.) | ISBN 9781532124013 (ebook) |
    ISBN 9781532124501 (Read-to-me ebook)
Subjects: LCSH: Harley-Davidson motorcycle--Juvenile literature. | Motorcycles--Juvenile literature. |
    Bikes--Juvenile literature. | Harley-Davidson motorcycle--History--Juvenile literature.
Classification: DDC 629.22750--dc23

Table of Contents

Harley-Davidson

Harley-Davidson is an American motorcycle company.

William Harley and
Arthur Davidson started
the company in 1903.
Davidson's two brothers
joined shortly after.

William Davidson   Walter Davidson

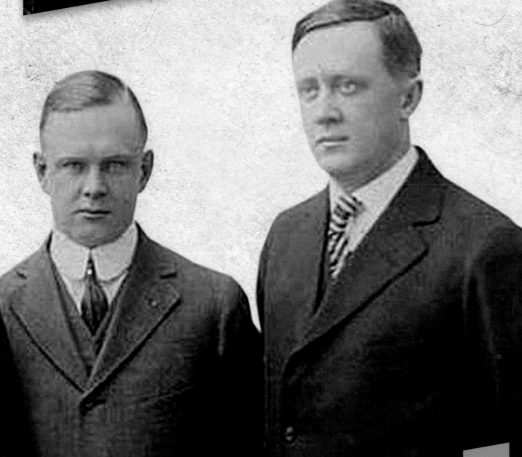

Arthur Davidson   William Harley

The first model was called Serial Number One. It was built to be a racer.

The EL model **debuted** in 1936. It was nicknamed the "Knucklehead" for the shape of its **rocker boxes**.

The FLHR Road King is very popular. It is fully equipped. It is great for long-distance rides.

The Look

Harley-Davidsons are cruising bikes. They are comfortable for long rides.

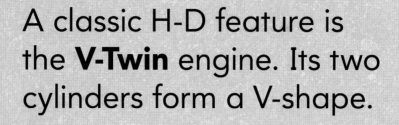

A classic H-D feature is the **V-Twin** engine. Its two cylinders form a V-shape.

Chrome **components** are found on many H-D motorcycles.

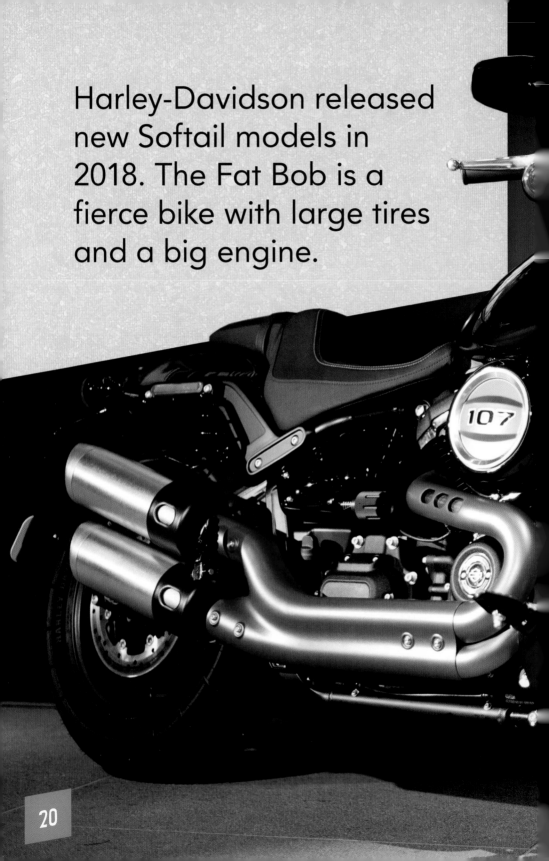

Harley-Davidson released new Softail models in 2018. The Fat Bob is a fierce bike with large tires and a big engine.

More Facts

- More than 700,000 bikers attend the Sturgis Motorcycle Rally each year. Many of them ride Harleys.

- The Harley-Davidson headquarters and museum are in Milwaukee, Wisconsin.

- Harley's Bar & Shield logo came out in 1910.

Glossary

components – parts.

debuted – the first appearance of something in public.

rocker box – a compartment that contains the mechanisms that control when and how much gas flows into an engine.

V-Twin – a two-cylinder internal combustion engine where the cylinders are arranged in a V-shape.

Index

Online Resources

Booklinks
NONFICTION NETWORK
FREE! ONLINE NONFICTION RESOURCES

To learn more about Harley-Davidson, please visit **abdobooklinks.com**. These links are routinely monitored and updated to provide the most current information available.